THE colour GARDEN

(yellow)

THE colour GARDEN

(yellow)

single colour plantings for dramatic landscapes

TEXT & PHOTOGRAPHY BY ELVIN MCDONALD
INTRODUCTION BY BRIDE M. WHELAN

LITTLE, BROWN AND COMPANY

BOSTON NEW YORK TORONTO LONDON

A LITTLE, BROWN BOOK

First published in Great Britain in 1997
by Little, Brown and Company (UK)

Conceived and produced by
Packaged Goods Incorporated
276 Fifth Avenue, New York, NY 10001
A Quarto Company

A CIP catalogue record for this book
is available from the British Library

ISBN 0-316-88235-6

10 9 8 7 6 5 4 3 2 1

Design by Stephen Fay
Endpapers by Michael Levine
Series Editor: Kristen Schilo
Colour separations by Wellmark Printing Press Limited
Printed in Hong Kong by Sing Cheong Printing Co. Ltd

UK companies, institutions and other organisations wishing to make bulk
purchases of this or any books published by Little, Brown should contact their
local bookshop or the Special Sales department at the address below.
Tel: 0171 911 8000 Fax: 0171 911 8100

Little, Brown and Company (UK)
Brettenham House, Lancaster Place
London WC2E 7EN

yellow's
for shining lights
and angels
Bonny and David
Larry and Lea
Janis B.
Betsy K.

Thanks to the gardens and gardeners who permitted me to photograph...

Barnsley House Gardens, England; John Brookes and Denman's Gardens, England; Brooklyn Botanic Garden, Brooklyn, NY; Francis Cabot, La Malbaie, Quebec; The Chelsea Flower Show, London; The Conservatory Gardens, Central Park, New York City; Descanso Gardens, La Canada Flintridge, CA; Great Dixter Gardens, England; C.Z. Guest, Palm Beach, FL; Hidcote Manor Garden, near Broadway, England; Hortus Bulborum, Heiloo, The Netherlands; Jasmine Hill Gardens, Montgomery, AL; Royal Botanical Gardens at Kew, London; Leonardslee Gardens, England; Lilypons Water Gardens, Brookshire, TX; Longwood Gardens, Kennett Square, PA; Meadowbrook Farms, Meadowbrook, PA; Mercer Arboretum & Botanic Gardens, Humble, TX; University of Minnesota Landscape Arboretum, Chanhassen; Moody Gardens, Galveston, TX; Museum of Garden History, Lambeth Church, London; National Wildflower Research Center, Austin, TX; The New York Botanical Garden, Bronx, NY; Old Westbury Gardens, Old Westbury, NY; Planting Fields Arboretum, Oyster Bay, NY; Plum Creek Farm, Sharon, CT; Sissinghurst Castle Gardens, England; Strybing Arboretum, San Francisco, CA; Upton House Gardens, England; Wakehurst Gardens, England; William Wheeler, New York City.

Rudbeckia fulgida 'Goldsturm'
is a cultivated form of black-eyed-
Susan with black-cone centres and
saturated yellow ray flowers.

contents

introduction

With yellow-orange and orange on its warm side and yellow-green and green on its cool side, yellow creates an array of endlessly moving patterns as well as dazzling shocks of colour. This vibrant hue carries the eye from one section of the garden to the other in an orderly flow, much like a musical score. The yellow garden is active. It is spontaneous, joyous, and warm.

Yellow is the first hue of early spring. The harsh browns of winter are lonely and unfriendly. Then, later, the yellow crocus bursts onto the landscape with astonishing contrast. Likewise, the yellow-green leaves of the willow tree, silhouetted against the grey spring sky are resplendent in their sway and lift the spirit.

Yellow's summer season begins with the showy brilliance of

the low marigold. The flaming orange and yellow daylilies *(pages 36 and 39)*; warm and sturdy zinnias; and finally, dusky orange California poppies *(page 38)* are all major players in the movement through the yellow palette during the course of summer.

The medium wavelength of definable colour is yellow. As light is radiant, visible energy, those flowers reflecting the colour yellow are the ultimate expressions of significant brightness and movement. To better understand yellow, think of the circular sun and moon. The circular brilliance of the yellow garden excites, rather than providing a place of comfort and repose. In a yellow-hued garden it is important for the eye to experience an occasional restful space. A dominant yellow garden is best as a walk-through garden with intersecting and divergent pathways, slicing through the yellow and harnessing its constant sense of movement.

The natural opposite of yellow on the colour wheel is violet or purple. The violet of the early spring crocus and variegated pansies, combined with the jutting iris, establish a perfect seasonal complement that does not impair or clash with the visual brilliance of yellows, such as lantana and gold coleus. The violets create a natural boundary in which yellow is controlled, allowing the eye to come to rest naturally.

BRIDE M. WHELAN

(I)

beds and borders

YELLOW IS FOR THE SUN. ITS RADIANCE IS THE GARDEN'S LIFE source. Through the centuries various yellow daisy flowers have been called "marigold," for Mary's gold, presumably the Virgin Mary. The Old World pot-marigold *(above)*, *Calendula officinalis*, flowers freely from spring till the first frost, in any expression of yellow, from pale cream to dark orange. The New World marigolds, developed from *Tagetes* native to Mexico, are choice for summer bedding—tiny-flowered, fern-leaved dwarf types used as edgers *(left)*, or any of a variety from knee- to chest-height, with flowers the size of large oranges.

Universally, loyalty and honour are associated with yellow. In the Southern Hemisphere the spring month of October is considered yellow; summer, yellow and blue; the autumn month of April, orange or gold.

Persian buttercups, the
Ranunculus of florists,
bloom in spring from tubers
set the previous autumn.
Besides purest yellow
(above), they come also in
white, orange, red, and pink.
Swatches of yellow pansies
(Viola) interspersed with
tall snapdragons
(Antirrhinum) in a formula
mixture that includes bright
yellow help celebrate the
season around a classic
water lily pool.

Surely one of the noblest yellows of the spring season is the peony, a bit surprising since the flower itself is so often equated with the ultimate in floral pinks, roses, reds, and whites.

One of the earliest flowering is the central Caucasus herbaceous species *P. mlokosewitschii*, with large, single, lemon-yellow flowers carried above tidy, knee-high clumps of bluish-green leaves. The flowers are followed in autumn by striking seed-pods.

The tree peony species *P. lutea* from western China represents the class of peonies referred to as the "King of Flowers" in China and the "Flower of Prosperity" in Japan. It was first brought to the West in the late 18th century by Sir Joseph Banks, who introduced it to the Royal Botanical Gardens at Kew, London. A more robust variety, *P.l. ludlowii*, has larger flowers. Hybrids include 'Chromatella,' with sulphur-yellow double flowers, and 'L'Esperance,' semi-double with a dark-blotched centre.

The herbaceous peony *Paeonia sterniana (above, left)* is a yellow-flowered species from southeast Tibet. The tree peony species *P. lutea* and cultivars *(above, right)* are among the spring border's most treasured yellow flowers for garden show and for cutting to bring indoors.

Paeonia mlokosewitschii, a yellow herbaceous species, highlights spring in "Mrs. Winthrop's Garden," an area at Hidcote Manor Garden, Gloucestershire. Named for the mother of its maker, Lawrence Johnston, it features mostly yellow and blue.

Golden rod is a North American wildflower that has been much improved through cultivation and the crossing, deliberate or by chance, of several species of *Solidago*. Named cultivars range from compact bushes barely knee-high to tall ones shoulder-height that need staking. Outstanding for golden yellow late summer and autumn.

American golden rod species and cultivars of *Solidago (opposite page)*, the European *Telekia speciosa (left, upper)*, and *Achillea filipendulina* 'Coronation Gold' *(left, lower)* are all hardy perennial members of the daisy family that bring an abundance of yellow to beds and borders from early summer through autumn.

The golden rods like well-drained soil and will tolerate shade but do best in full sun. An interesting companion is × *Solidaster luteus*, an intergeneric hybrid between *Solidago* and *Aster*, with small daisy-flowers instead of the fluffy panicles of golden rod.

Telekia's leaves are mostly at the base of the plant, so that the distinctive yellow daisy flowers stand out boldly at shoulder height. It likes sun or shade but needs moist soil: it suits a pond-side. This perennial from southeastern Europe to the south of Russia may bloom the first year from seeds.

The achilleas offer a treasure chest of different yellows, from creamy to deep gold on ferny-leaved plants that hug the ground or (like 'Coronation Gold') can grow more than waist- high. Late spring to mid-summer is their time; sunny, dry conditions favour healthier leaves.

🌿 Golden variegated hakone grass (*Hakonechloa macra* 'Aureola') turns its most vivid yellow in a balance of direct sun and shade.

The ornamental grasses include several with yellow or golden leaves, the Japanese *Hakonechloa macra* 'Aureola' or golden variegated hakone grass being one of the most obvious. It grows close to the ground, the lightly green-streaked leaves arching over each other in the manner of overlapping shingles.

Two varieties of the popular *Miscanthus sinensis* are distinctively—and similarly—cross-banded with evenly spaced yellow markings along the leaves, the main differences being that porcupine grass (*M.s.* var. *strictus*) is upright and more cold-tolerant than the more lax zebra grass (*M.s.* 'Zebrinus'). The best view of them is early or late in the day with back or cross lighting.

Other yellow grasses or grass-like plants: *Acorus gramineus* 'Ogon' (golden variegated sweet flag), *Alopecurus pratensis* var. *aureus* (yellow foxtail), and *Carex elata* 'Bowles Golden' (a sedge).

🌿 Zebra grass, *Miscanthus sinensis* 'Zebrinus' *(opposite)*, with gracefully arching yellow-banded leaves, and the similar porcupine grass, *M. s.* var. *strictus*, with spikier, more upright leaves, are best appreciated by watching as wind currents set in motion their sun and shade patterns.

🦅 *Laburnum* x *watereri* 'Vossii' is an outstanding yellow-flowered tree for small gardens. It is most famous for training over an arboured walkway so that the yellow flowers through mid-spring show off to their best advantage, such as in the Queen's Garden *(right)* at Kew Gardens. Inside, the theme is pure gold; beds immediately outside the arbour bloom at the same time with English bluebells *(Hyacinthoides).*

Shrubs with yellow leaves can stand out in beds and borders in the same way as flowers. There are numerous euonymus with evergreen leaves variously edged, margined, or coloured entirely with yellow, from creamy to vivid; some can be almost too assertive in the landscape unless deftly mixed with yellow flowers or counter-balanced by bright to deep blues and blue-green leaves.

A yellow-variegated English holly (*Ilex*) trimmed to cone shape stands at the centre of Tradescant's Garden *(left, upper)*, behind Lambeth Church in London, emphasising the yellow blooms of *Inula* and *Asphodelus* and complementing the blue of German iris. The holly leaves also play up the pale green of the box *(Buxus)* hedges.

Common privet (*Ligustrum ovalifolium*) and its variety 'Aureum,' golden privet, are sometimes planted together and sheared into topiaries like this globe in a Japanese garden *(left, middle)*, or into bicoloured hedging, sheared or informal.

'Goldflame' *Spiraea japonica* is a twiggy small shrub that is coppery early in spring, then bright, glowing yellow-green at tulip time *(left, lower)*, followed by a covering of pink flowers. Prune when they fade, removing entirely the oldest wood and the dead blooms from the strong young branches.

Large-flowered hybrid roses such as the grandiflora 'Gold Medal' *(left)* and the hybrid tea 'King's Ransom' *(below)*, along with the smaller, cluster-flowered 'Goldilocks,' a floribunda, are a reliable source of glowing yellow—and rose scent—from the first blooms of summer until frost.

*T*he Austrian briar or Austrian yellow rose, *Rosa foetida*, brought to the West from Asia by the 16th century, has played an important role in the development of the yellow rose, climbers like the one trained on a brick cottage wall *(opposite, upper),* as well as shrub and bush types. The double-flowered *R.f. persiana* (Persian yellow rose), crossed with a red-flowered hybrid perpetual seedling in 1900, produced 'Soleil d'Or,' the first large-flowered modern hybrid tea that was yellow.

Another yellow species variety, *R. banksiae* 'Lutea,' the yellow Banksian rose *(opposite, lower),* is a thornless Chinese evergreen that puts forth one burst of spring bloom in milder climates. There is also the hardier, shrubbier *R.* x *harisonii*, or Harison's Yellow. The very recent English rose 'Graham Thomas' is everblooming, soft yellow, fragrant.

(2)

water garden

*I*F EVER SUNBEAMS DANCE IN A GARDEN, IT IS WHEN THE PALE
lemon water lilies *(Nymphaea)* are blooming *(opposite),* or the creamy sacred
lotus blossom *(Nelumbo),* having risen up from a seemingly mucky grave, stands
above undulating, curving leaves, radiant in the shimmering light. As the flower
begins to age, the bold, primitive seed receptacle appears *(above).* This juxtaposi-
tion emphasises the contrast between the ephemeral petals and leaves and the
life-giving, edible seeds that also perpetuate the plant.

There are many yellow-flowered plants suited to water gardening. Water lily
and lotus grow from pots of earth submerged in a pond or pool, with the roots
and lower plant parts underwater. The water poppy *(Hydrocleys nymphoides),* grows
on the water surface with lemon-yellow flowers, brown stamens, and a light scent.

Besides the grass-like New Zealand flax *(Phormium)*, which has spikes of bright yellow flowers in warm climates and thrives in the constantly moist but drained soil of a pond or stream bank, there are also some grass-like plants with yellow leaves for setting in similarly wet spots: golden variegated sweet flag *(Acorus gramineus* 'Ogon') and Bowles' golden sedge *(Carex elata* 'Aurea'). True grasses for planting in close proximity to water are gold-variegated gardeners' garters *(Phalaris arundinacea* 'Luteo-Picta') and creamy yellow-striped giant reed grass *(Phragmites australis* 'Variegatus').

Plants that grow wild in boggy or swampy ground can sometimes make bold statements in the yellow garden. An aroid native to western North America called skunk cabbage *(Lysichiton americanum),* for the smell of its flowers and the plant's appearance, is fully hardy. It grows in wet-to-moist humusy soil, leafing out and flowering in spring before companion plants interfere, especially the appearance of leaves on deciduous trees and shrubs, which change the "cabbage" plant's sunny spring warmth to cool summer shade. Besides the handsome leaves, the boat-shaped, pale-to-bright-yellow spathe part of the blossom is large enough to be appreciated at some distance. The 'Aurea' form of creeping Jenny, *Lysimachia nummularia,* is a suitable gold-leaved companion.

Grass-like New Zealand flax *(Phormium)* grows on a mild-climate pond bank *(above)* where the roots have a constant water source but conditions are not always boggy.

Lysichiton americanum (opposite), for bogs or swamp gardens, has pale yellow, boat-shaped spathes in the spring.

The marsh marigold (Caltha palustris) is suited to planting in boggy ground or up to a hand's width deep in water. Bright yellow buttercup-like flowers appear in spring. A double-flowered form, 'Flore Pleno,' has graced gardens since the 17th century.

The yellow flag, *Iris pseudacorus* *(right)*, originally from Europe and North Africa, is cultivated in gardens over most of the world. It has also successfully colonized many wet sites— ditches, bogs, pond and stream banks—and is one of the tougher plants that produces showy yellow flowers every spring and early summer without fail. Deadheading will keep self-sown seedlings from becoming a nuisance, but clumps do spread. There is also a yellow-and-green-leaved form, 'Variegata,' that is most dramatic in spring before it blooms. *I.p.* 'Flore Pleno' has double flowers. The paler, primrose-yellow variety *I.p. bastardii* is rather less vigorous than the species.

Suited to similarly wet or boggy ground are the tender Louisiana iris such as yellow 'Dixie Deb'. These elegant flowers and relatively graceful, grassy plants are worth trying to grow where winter cold is neither extreme nor protracted.

(3)

spring yellows

T NO TIME IS YELLOW SO MUCH APPRECIATED AS WHEN IT appears at the beginning of spring, thereby signalling the end of a dark, cold, even dreary time, and the dawning of an exuberant, expansive season. Golden crocus and green-ruffed yellow buttercup-like winter aconite *(Eranthis)* are harbingers that come out in winter at the merest hint of spring, to be followed by major players: primroses *(Primula)* from greenish- to reddish-yellow *(above)* and tulips *(Tulipa)* from the small yellow-and-white species *T. tarda* to the regal Darwin such as 'Golden Apeldoorn' *(opposite)*.

Perhaps no yellow of spring is more coveted than that of a bright golden, fragrant daffodil *(Narcissus)* such as 'King Alfred' or 'Unsurpassable.' The genus is as rich in garden yellows for spring as *Hemerocallis* (daylily) is for summer.

Common broom *(Cytisus scoparius)* has about as much gold in its gene bank as any spring-flowering shrub. Some are so richly saturated the colour can be blinding on a sunny day. The paler to lemon-yellow selections *(opposite, upper)* have more subtlety for small gardens; they can look their best in mixed company with a strong yellow tulip such as the lily-flowered 'West Point' or the green-stitched, frilled and shirred 'Yellow Parrot.'

Gold dust alyssum *(opposite,* lemon, with white perennial candytuft, *Iberis sempervirens)*, like the broom, can vary from rich egg-yolk tones to paler lemon tints, the latter more easily worked into a theme of pastels for a spring rock garden or wall planting. Ordinary gold dust *(Aurinia saxatilis)* can be toned down by placing it next to spring whites such as candytuft, arabis, *Anemone blanda,* and Roman hyacinths *(Hyacinthus orientalis ablulus)*.

Other herbaceous perennial spring yellows include celandine poppy *(Stylophorum)*, native to the eastern United States, for partly shaded, wild plantings and leopard's bane *(Doronicum)*, for pointing up yellow, blue, or white bulbs. *Corydalis, Chiastophyllum* (indigenous to the Caucas Mountain area of Southeast Asia) and selected *Cheiranthus, Erysimum,* and *Viola* can be the source for more spring yellows, especially for rock gardens, rock walls, massing by steps, and at the front of taller plantings, and for mixing or matching in pots.

The fabled orange crown imperial immortalized in Flemish paintings by the Dutch masters is also available in varieties having yellow bell flowers, such as *Fritillaria imperialis* 'Lutea Maxima' *(above)* and the western North American native *F. pudica* or yellow bell. These bulbs are for temperate gardens and spring blooms. Swift drainage is needed and dry soil in summer.

Corylopsis, a small genus of shrubs from Japan, blooms early, before its leaves come out. They, the witch hazels *(Hamamelis),* and the unusual *Stachyurus,* are among the season's earliest yellow flowers. The Cornelian cherry, *Cornus mas,* is another, a sturdy, self-reliant shrub that can grow into a tidy tree.

Trees for spring include weeping willows for yellow effect, yellow magnolias such as 'Elizabeth,' and the golden chain *(Laburnum).* Gardeners in warm regions can also grow fragrant, puffy, golden acacias, golden trumpet tree *(Tabebuia),* and yellow bells *(Tecoma).*

Yellow foliage is also another source for this colour in the spring landscape. In addition to the previously mentioned *Euonymus* and the gold-variegated forms of holly *(Ilex)* there is the golden-leaved Japanese maple *(Acer japonicum* 'Aureum'), such oaks as *Quercus rubra* 'Aurea' and *Gleditsia triacanthos* 'Sunburst,' a honey locust with delicate, ferny leaves which are golden yellow at first.

Corylopsis pauciflora, (above, with 'King Alfred' daffodils) is one of several shrubs that bloom at the very beginning of spring, before it comes into leaf. Greenish bracts hold the sweetly scented yellow flowers of *C. spicata.*

A golden oak of garden origin, *Quercus rubra* 'Aurea' *(opposite),* lights up a rainy day.

(4)

summer and autumn golds

𝒴ELLOW SUMMER FLOWERS HOLD ON TO THEIR COLOUR EVEN in brilliant light. Among annuals the *Helianthus* sunflowers *(above)* are favoured for garden show and cutting. Foremost among perennials are yellow daylilies *(opposite)* available in thousands of different cultivars. Their botanical genus is *Hemerocallis*, whose genes predispose yellow, gold, and orange; their genius lies with breeders who have coaxed from them every colour in the floral rainbow —including white—except clear blue. By the cooler days of autumn, most of the garden's yellows will have deepened to gold, a warm colour found in chrysanthemum, African marigold *(Tagetes)*, pot-marigold *(Calendula)*, and *Rudbeckia*.

The narrow-leaf zinnia (*Z. angustiflora* or *linearis)* comes in yellow, gold, and white varieties. It can be summer ground cover in sun or permitted to scramble over the side of a window box. It tolerates long, hot summers and needs little care.

California poppies (*Eschscholzia)* in their native state are usually this colour, a soft orange. There are also hybrids varying from creamy to salmon, some pastel, some in vivid hues. They prosper in full sun and well-drained soil.

The tawny daylily has spread so successfully on its own and with the help of admiring gardeners, the species is considered weedy by *Hemerocallis* devotees. In the right place, such as by a dark-painted holiday house, it is ideal, self-reliant, and completely carefree.

Basic yellow, gold and orange are clearly expressed in the marigolds of summer and autumn. They can be single or double, dwarf or tall; you can choose cultivars in a single hue or mixtures in blending shades. Pot-marigolds (*Calendula*) range in impact from the cottage-garden simplicity of a single daisy-flower to the sophistication of a multi-petalled chrysanthemum. Double French and African marigolds (*Tagetes*) resemble a carnation in shape. Thriving in summer heat, their golden tones glow best beside silver leaves such as artemisia 'Powis Castle', and look most intense on a grey day.

Coleus 'Fairway Yellow' and 'Pineapple Wizard' grow into knee-high bushes made up entirely of bright lime-green and yellow leaves, with best colour developing in half-day or more direct sun.

Some additional sources for yellow among annuals for summer and autumn: sulphur cosmos 'Bright Lights,' *Chrysanthemum* 'Moonlight,' *Dahlia* 'Sunny Yellow,' California poppy (*Eschscholzia*), *Gazania* 'Talent,' sunflower (*Helianthus*), petunia 'Carpet Buttercream,' and many zinnias, from the profuse, small-flowered, narrow-leaf (*Z. linearis*) to the larger saucer-size 'Dreamland Yellow.'

The florists' 'mum', hybrids
of Chrysanthemum
morifolium,—above, in a
pale yellow, with slightly
incurved, quilled petals—has
been cultivated for thousands
of years. It also has several
garden relatives — annuals
and perennials — in every
yellow imaginable. Sulphur
cosmos 'Bright Lights'
(right) blooms summer-
autumn, ideal for the garden
and cutting.

🖎   *Potentilla fruticosa* becomes
a woody perennial with yellow
flowers all summer. Blanket-flower
Gaillardia (foreground) can be
annual or perennial, with a long
season of reddish-yellow,
bicoloured, or red blooms.

A summer-planted, hardy bulb, *Sternbergia lutea* announces the arrival of autumn with its chrome-yellow, crocus-like flowers that sprout up almost overnight in early autumn and bloom on naked stems. Since the leaves appear in spring, then disappear, a summer companion is needed, such as orange impatiens (*shown*), or a carpeting yellow-leaved plant such as golden thyme (*Thymus*).

🌱 'Little Aurora' hosta's lime-yellow leaves stand out in a garden even at night. Dusky violet-blue flowers appear in summer. 'Kabitan,' another small hosta, has yellow-green lance leaves with a narrow dark green edge.

🌱 'Gold Standard' hosta is one of the garden's most dramatic yellow-leaved perennials. The reverse of its colour pattern is seen in 'Aurora Borealis,' whose large, quilted leaves are flamed yellow-green at the edges, highlighting the powdery, blue-green centres.

The yellows and golds of summer reach a crescendo in autumn, an earthly response to the waning of the sun's rays. Dahlias, roses, and chrysanthemums stand out in these colours but it is when trees and shrubs start to turn yellow overnight—aspen, poplar, ginkgo, *Lindera obtusiloba*—that the changing of the seasons becomes official. It takes a sharp eye to spot them amongst the dying leaves, but there they are: tiny, ribbony, yellow witch hazel flowers from *Hamamelis virginiana*, possibly the latest woody plant to bloom in temperate climates.

Besides all the sources of yellow flowers and leaves mentioned specifically in these pages, here are the clues for spotting such plants in a listing of botanical names: *auratus* (golden, gold-coloured); *aureo-* (prefix meaning golden); *aureus, -a, -um* (golden); *flavescens* (yellowish; becoming yellow); *flavi-* (prefix meaning yellow); *flavus, -a, -um* (yellow); *luteolus, -a, -m* (yellowish); *lutescens* (becoming yellowish); *luteus, -a, -um* (yellow).

Impatiens hawkeri, a species from New Guinea, has passed its genes for golden leaves on to a generation of hybrids *(above)* with large, showy flowers and brightly variegated foliage. This low branching impatiens of the sultana type has clear, golden-centred leaves and pink to tangerine flowers.

(5)

complementary colour schemes

Y ELLOW'S OPPOSITE ON THE COLOUR WHEEL IS VIOLET, GOLD'S (or yellow-orange's) is blue-violet, orange's is blue, and yellow-green's is red-violet. Mixed or matched, these are highly complementary—for example yellow and orange English wallflowers *(Cheiranthus)* with blue *Myosotis* forget-me-nots *(opposite)* for spring, or the same complementary colours in summer from a host of yellow and orange daylilies *(Hemerocallis)* and blue *Aster, Campanula,* and *Veronica.*

Another approach to developing a complementary colour scheme is to repeat the colours in a single blossom, a bicoloured tulip such as 'Helmar' *(above),* for example, a Rembrandt with red-violet feathering in a field of creamy yellow.

Yellow-and-white as a garden colour scheme might be taken from any number of dahlias, from those whose deep yellow petals are merely tipped in white to those with so much white they are cream yellow. The Shasta daisy, with white rays and golden disks, is often used with pinks and blues—roses, delphiniums—but try it with lime lady's-mantle *(Alchemilla),* yellow-leaved spirea, and a golden sage *(Salvia).*

No season is without its quota of yellow and white flowers, but considering their potentially cooling effect by day, and their luminosity which can be appreciated on moonlit walks, summer seems ideal. The city terrace container garden *(right)* includes some prime players for a mating of yellow *(Coreopsis, Rudbeckia)* and white ('White Swan' *Echinacea,* white *Liatris).* The sunflowers *(Helianthus)* are a major source for yellow, or even white ('Italian White'). Hollyhocks *(Althea)* come in both colours, as do achillea, *Deutzia scabra* 'Candidissima,' yucca, honeysuckle *(Lonicera),* and jasmine *(Jasminum).*

A half-round wooden planter for a city terrace is filled with *Coreopsis verticillata* 'Moonbeam,' *Echinacea* 'White Swan,' golden-glow *(Rudbeckia laciniata* 'Hortensia'), and white *Liatris.*

Snowy, fragrant, white Dutch hyacinths and bright yellow 'Peeping Tom' daffodils *(Narcissus)* are enhanced by a dreamy go-between: white and pale yellow 'Ice Follies' daffodil.

Lemon-yellow and cherry-red tulips set the colour scheme for a spring garden.

Primary yellow and red together in a garden can be cheery or even brash *(above)*. Deep yellow and harmonious shades of gold, mixed with warm reds, make for a rich effect easily attained in spring with tulips and other bulbs, wallflower *(Cheiranthus)*, and pansy *(Viola)*, later from a host of annuals and perennials, and finally, in autumn, the hardy chrysanthemums, whose family is generously endowed in this range.

A number of daisy-flowered perennials that combine gold and red-mahogany in one flower include *Ratibida,* or Mexican-hat (there is also a form that is entirely golden yellow), blanket-flower *(Gaillardia),* and numerous annual *Tagetes* of the French marigold type. These plants will produce blooms all summer.

Bright yellow lantanas, in training as tree-form standards, grow as giant lollipops from a bed of red *Begonia semperflorens*. There is also a pale yellow lantana and one whose flowers can be yellow, orange, and red all at once. Blue sage and yellow marigolds grow in the background. All bloom best in sun.

The colour yellow is curiously missing—or mostly so—from the always-in-bloom bedding begonia, *B. semperflorens*, yet its many shades of red, from rosy to almost orange, get on well with yellow flowers such as lantana and foliages such as gold coleus. Each blossom—if it is of the single type—has a prominent display of yellow-to-golden colour at its centre: scintillating clusters of pollen grains if it is the male, pronged and minutely haired receptacles if the female. Evergreen *B. sempervirens* is usually grown as a half-hardy annual. Yellow is well represented, however, among Multiflora and Pendula cultivars of another begonia, *B.* × *tuberhybrida*, with sumptuous dangling flowers that show particularly well in hanging baskets.

Creamy yellow spires of *Baptisia* stand out in front of dark red wallflower *(Cheiranthus)*. The soft yellows can serve as accents or for blending darker and lighter shades. Later, when the baptisia has finished, the potentilla behind and hybrid lilies *(Lilium)* will add bright yellow to this part of the garden.

The drama of a red-and-yellow scheme can be heightened by the range of shades used. A pale or lemony yellow such as from a cultivar of hardy herbaceous perennial *Baptisia (left)* has the power to make the other colours appear more deeply brilliant.

By contrast, a high note expressed in a clear lipstick red, such as small-flowered but profuse and long-blooming *Salvia greggii* can have a magical effect in playing up the darker, more vivid yellows such as from *Coreopsis* 'Early Sunrise,' gold-and-mahogany French marigold *(Tagetes)*, and *Berberis thunbergii* 'Atropurpurea Nana' *(opposite)*.

The yellow-and-red team also includes purple fountain grass *(Pennisetum)*, purple perilla, and 'Purple Ruffles' basil *(Ocimum)*. The herb known as bronze fennel *(Foeniculum vulgare* 'Purpureum') combines reddish leaves all season that are crowned by late summer with umbels of tiny yellow flowers.

Tulip yellow and forget-me-not blue is one of nature's most ubiquitous complementary colour schemes, a floral mirror to sunbeams and blue skies. A similar effect might be achieved in summer by placing in a bed of yellow flowers a large blue-and-white ceramic pot.

Velvety bright yellow and gleaming mahogany pansies in an antique concrete urn affirm the synergy of yellow and red together, in this case a red so saturated with colour it is reddish-brown.

PHAL. PARTY DRE
× BARBARA MOLE

PHAL. BARBARA MOLE

PAPH. A MENI

(6)

w a r m   c l i m a t e   y e l l o w s

Yellow's relative colourfastness favours its popularity in warm-climate landscapes. Moreover, many plants native to the tropics have disproportionately large golden flowers, such as in selections of Chinese hibiscus *(above)*, or an extraordinary appearance, as in the yellow ladyslipper orchids *(opposite)* of noble bearing. The climbing *Solandra*, from Central America and the West Indies, is called "golden chalice" for the colour and shape of its blossoms, as wide as a dinner plate. One cultivar of *Solandra maxima* also has creamy yellow-variegated foliage. Croton *(Codiaeum)* can be a shrub or small tree with green-veined, bright yellow leaves. You can find yellow-leafed cultivars of *Dieffenbachia*, as well as yellow *Sansevieria* 'Golden Hahnii,' yellow bloodleaf *(Iresine lindenii)* and yellow parrot leaf *(Alternanthera ficoidea* 'Aurea').

Yellow oleander *(left)* is *Thevetia peruviana*, with tea-rose scented flowers any time it has sun, heat, and water. The plant is an evergreen shrub or small tree.

Hummingbirds favour the intricate yellow flowers of *Passiflora citrina (above, upper),* in the American tropics. Golden trumpet-vine *(above, lower)* is *Allamanda cathartica* 'Hendersonii.' It can be shrubby or a huge vine.

Yellow king's-crown or Brazilian plume (*Justicia aurea*), native to Mexico and Central America, shows off its feathery plumes in warm conditions, silhouetted (*right*) dramatically against a dark background. Justicia can be cut back and carried through winter in a moderately warm, frost-free place.

Yellow shrimp plant, *Justicia brandegeana* 'Yellow Queen,' has long-lasting lemon-yellow bracts from which the ephemeral white flowers are borne. In the related *Pachystachys lutea*, or lollipop plant, the bracts are held decidedly upright and they are a richer, golden yellow that almost glows.

Columnea, a genus of upright or trailing gesneriads, includes several yellows that bloom constantly in warm, moist, brightness, outdoors or in, such as 'Top Brass' and 'Yellow Dragon.'

The yellow calla lily, *Zantedeschia elliottiana*, is a regal flower for growing in summer pots or beds. During this active time the tuberous roots need a constant supply of water, but in winter they can be kept nearly dry and in the dark.

The orchid family glitters with gold among the butterfly and dancing-lady yellows in the genus *Oncidium* (*right, upper*). *Anguloa clowesii*, the cradle orchid, is bright yellow, and so too the tulip cattleya, *C. citrina*, and many different species of *Dendrobium*.

Yellow-flowered trees can be prominent in mild-climate gardens, such as the fragrant *Acacia* (*right, lower*), golden-bell *Tabebuia argentea*, golden trumpet-tree *T. chrysotricha*, and ylang-ylang (*Cananga odorata*) with ribbony yellow flowers treasured for their sweet-smelling perfume.

Two members of the pea family, *Cassia* and *Senna*, contain showy yellow-flowering shrubs and trees. While many are for warm climates, wild senna (*Cassia marilandica*) is hardier.

Notable yellow-flowered vines for warm gardens include *Merremia tuberosa* (wood-rose), *Hibbertia scandens* (guinea flower or snake), and *Stigmaphyllon ciliatum* with frilly blooms followed by showy, butterfly-shaped green seeds.

Dancing lady and butterfly orchids (*Oncidium*) bloom yellow over a long season (*above*).

Acacia contains a host of arid, warm-climate trees (*below*) and shrubs, outstanding for their yellow, unique perfume, and the florist cut flower called "mimosa."

stockists

Acton Beauchamp Roses
Acton Beauchamp
Worcester
Hereford & Worcester WR6 5AE
tel (01531) 640433
wide range of roses

Allwood Bros
Hassocks
West Sussex BN6 9NB
Tel (01273) 844229
dianthus family: plants & seed

Jacques Amand Ltd
The Nurseries
145 Clamp Hill
Stanmore
Middlesex HA7 3JS
Tel (0181) 9548138
species bulbs

David Austin Roses Ltd
Bowling Green Lane
Albrighton
Wolverhampton
West Midlands WV7 3HB
Tel (01902) 373931
*roses, peony, hemerocallis, iris &
other herbaceous plants*

Avon Bulbs
Burnt House Farm
mid-Lambrook
South Petherton
Somerset TA13 5HE
Tel (01460) 242177
smaller & unusual bulbs

Ballyrogan Nurseries
The Grange
Ballyrogan
Newtownards
Co Down
Northern Ireland BT23 6QB
Tel (01247) 810451
*agapanthus, euphorbia, geranium,
iris, meconopsis & other perennials;
shrubs*

Peter Beales Roses
London Road
Attleborough
Norfolk NR17 1AY
Tel (01953) 454707
old-fashioned roses

Binny Plants
West Lodge
Binny Estate
Ecclesmachen Road
near Broxbourn
West Lothian EH52 6NL
Tel (01506) 858931
herbaceous, alpines, shrubs etc

Blackmore & Langdon Ltd
Pensford
Bristol
Avon BS18 4JL
Tel (01275) 332300
perennials

**Bressingham Gardens Mail
Order**
Bressingham, Diss
Norfolk IP22 2AB
Tel (01379) 687468
very wide range

Brook Farm
Boulson Lane
Newent
Gloucestershire GL18 1JH
Tel (01531) 822534
unusual hardy plants

Burnside Nursery
by Girvan
Ayrshire KA26 9JH
Tel (01465) 714290
*dicentra, hardy geraniums; plants &
seed*

The Beth Chatto Gardens Ltd
Elmstead Market
Colchester
Essex CO7 7DB
Tel (01206) 822007
*herbaceous plants, esp. unusual
species*

Chiltern Seeds
Bortree Stile
Ulverston
Cumbria LA12 7PB
Tel (01229) 581137
wide range of seeds

Paul Christian Rare Plants
PO Box 468
Wrexham
Clwyd LL13 9XR
Tel (01978) 366399
bulbs, corms, tubers

Christie's Nursery
Downfield
Westmuir, Kirriemuir
Angus DD8 5LP
Tel (01575) 572977
alpines

Cilwern Plants
Cilwern
Talley
Carmarthenshire SA19 7YH
Tel (01558) 685526
hardy perennials

Collectors Corner Plants
33 Rugby Road
Clifton-under-Dunsmore
Rugby
Warwickshire CV23 0DE
Tel (01788) 571881
perennials and shrubs

The Cottage Herbery
Mill House
Boraston
near Tenbury Wells
Worcestershire WR15 8LZ
Tel (01584) 871575
herbs & foliage plants; seeds

Craig Lodge Nurseries
Balmaclellan
Castle Douglas
Kirkcudbrightshire DG7 3QR
Tel (01644) 420661
alpines, bulbs, rhododendrons

Deelish Garden Centre
Skibbereen
Co Cork
Republic of Ireland
Tel 00 353 (0)28 21374
*unusual plants, conservatory
plants, seeds*

Samuel Dobie & Sons Ltd
Broomhill Way
Torquay
Devon TQ2 7QW
Tel (01803) 616281
flowers and bulbs

Jack Drake
Inshriach Alpine Nursery
Aviemore
Invernessshire PH22 1QS
Tel (01540) 651287
alpines & rock plants & seed

Fairy Lane Nurseries
Fairy Lane, Sale
Greater Manchester M33 2JT
Tel (0161) 9051137
hardy & tender perennials, shrubs

**The Margery Fish Plant
Nursery**
East Lambrook Manor
East Lambrook
South Petherton
Somerset TA13 5HL
Tel (01460) 240328
*perennials: geranium, hellebore,
penstemon, salvia etc*

Mr Fothergill's Seeds Ltd
Gazeley Road
Kentford
Newmarket
Suffolk CB8 7QB
Tel (01638) 751161
wide range of flower seed

Garden Cottage Nursery
Tournaig, Poolewe
Achnasheen
Highland IV22 2LH
Tel (01445) 781339
herbaceous, alpines, shrubs

Glenhirst Cactus Nursery
Station Road
nr Boston
Lincolnshire PE20 3NX
Tel (01205) 820314
*cacti, succulent plants & seed;
desert plants*

Greenshoots Nursery
18 Sheppards Close
St Albans
Hertfordshire AL3 5AL
Tel (01727) 857152
perennials & shrubs

Hartside Nursery Garden
near Alston
Cumbria CA9 3BL
Tel (01434) 381372
*alpines, primulas, gentians,
meconopsis*

Hillview Hardy Plants
Worfield
near Bridgnorth
Shropshire WV15 5NT
Tel (01746) 716454
hardy perennials, alpines; seed

Holden Clough Nursery
Holden
Bolton-by-Bowland
Clitheroe
Lancashire BB7 4PF
Tel (01200) 447615
perennials; alpines; seed

Hopleys Plants Ltd
High Street
Much Hadham
Hertfordshire SG10 6BU
Tel (01279) 842509
*hardy & half-hardy shrubs &
perennials*

Houghton Farm Plants
Houghton
Arundel
West Sussex BN18 9LW
Tel (01798) 831327
*euphorbia, geranium, unusual
herbaceous*

W E Th Ingwersen Ltd
Birch Farm Nursery
Gravetye
East Grinstead
West Sussex RH19 4LE
Tel (01342) 810 236
*perennials, alpines, rock garden
plants & seed*

Kelways Nurseries
Langport
Somerset TA10 9SL
Tel (01458) 250521
*iris, peony, hemerocallis & other
perennials*

Knoll Gardens
Hampreston
Stapehill
near Wimborne
Dorset BH21 7ND
Tel (01202) 873931
*herbaceous plants, ceanothus,
phygelius*

Lakes' Hardy Plants
4 Fearns Building
Penistone
Sheffield S30 6BA
Tel (01226) 370574
unusual herbaceous

Mackey's Garden Centre
Castlepark Road
Sandycove
Co. Dublin
Republic of Ireland
Tel 00 353-1-2807385
*roses, shrubs, houseplants, alpines;
seed*

MGW Plants
45 Potovens Lane
Lofthouse Gate
Wakefield
YorkshireWF3 3JE
Tel (01924) 820096
alpines, bulbs, herbaceous

Old Manor Nurseries
South Leverton
Retford
Nottinghamshire DN22 0BX
Tel (01427) 880428
hardy perennials

Orchardstown Nurseries
Cork Road
Waterford
Republic of Ireland
Tel 00 353 (0)513 84273
*hardy plants, roses, shrubs,
climbers etc*

The Palm Farm
Thornton Hall Gardens
Station Road
Thornton Curtis
near Ulceby
Humberside DN39 6XF
Tel (01469) 531232
*palms, shrubs & conservatory
plants*

Plants Direct
19 William Street
Brynna
Pontyclun
Glamorganshire CF7 9QJ
Tel (01446) 793343
*hebe, penstemon & other shrubs &
perennials*

Plantworld
Burnham Road
South Woodham Ferrers
Chelmsford
Essex CM3 5QP
Tel (01245) 320482
hardy plants

Rose Tree Cottage Plants
Popes Hill
Newnham-on-Severn
Gloucestershire GL14 1JX
Tel (01594) 826692
alpines, herbaceous, unusual shrubs

**Scotts Nurseries
(Merriott) Ltd**
Merriott
Somerset TA16 5PL
Tel (01460) 72306
trees, shrubs, climbers, roses

Southview Nurseries
Chequers Lane
Eversley Cross
Basingstoke
Hampshire RG27 0NT
Tel (01734) 732206
*unusual & old-fashioned
perennials*

Stapeley Water Gardens Ltd
London Road
Stapeley
Nantwich
Cheshire CW5 7LH
Tel (01270) 623868
*waterlilies, aquatic & poolside
plants*

Suttons Seeds Ltd
Hele Road
Torquay
Devon TQ2 7QJ
Tel (01803) 614455
*bulbs, plants, wide range flower
seed*

Thompson & Morgan
London Road
Ipswich
Suffolk IP2 0BA
Tel (01473) 688821
wide range seed

Unwins Seeds Ltd
Histon
Cambridge CB4 4ZZ
Tel (01945) 588522
wide range seed, especially sweet pea

Upcott Nursery
Upcott
Morchard Bishop
Crediton
Devon EX17 6NG
Tel (01363) 877258
perennials

Van Tubergen UK Ltd
Bressingham, Diss
Norfolk IP22 2AB
Tel (01379) 688282
bulbs

Walled Garden Nursery
Helwith Cottage
Marske, Richmond
North Yorkshire DL11 7EG
Tel (01748) 884774
herbaceous plants

Waterwheel Nursery
Bully Hole Bottom
Usk Road
Shirenewton
Chepstow
Gwent NP6 6SA
Tel (01291) 641577
unusual trees, shrubs, perennials

index